REMARKABLE ROSE

Based on a true story
Kibera, Kenya 2002

Written by Ellie Roscher
Illustrated by Lily Banning

Rose **LOVED** soccer.

She loved to kick.

She loved to run.

She loved to play.

But in Kibera, girls didn't play soccer.

Rose walked to the dirt and pebble pitch and watched the boys playing.

When she tried to join them, an older boy snatched the ball from her and spit, "Go home, girl, and help your momma in the kitchen!"

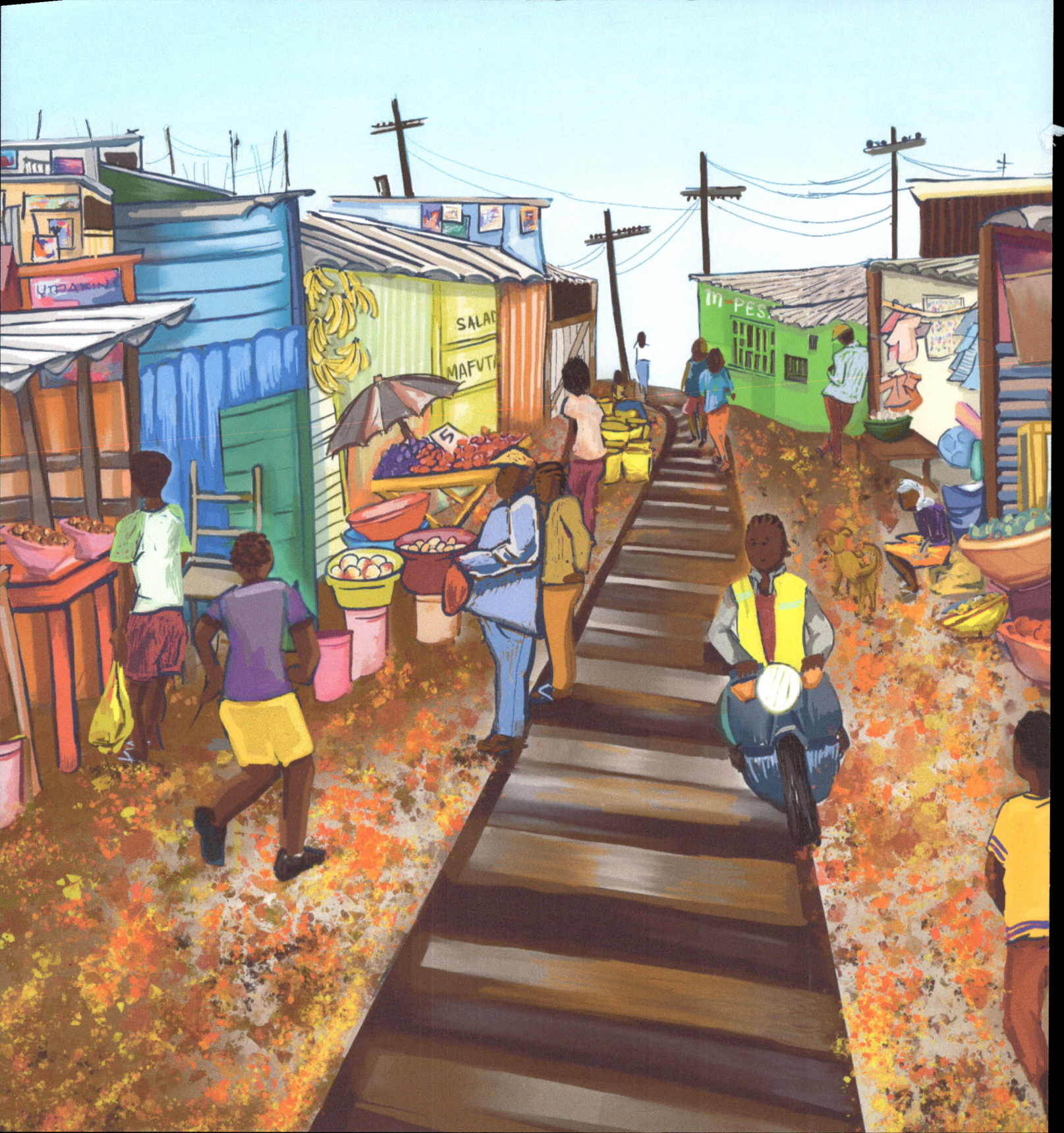

Rose stomped off toward home, frowning.

She paused at the *kibanda* by her house so she could peek at the women from other countries playing soccer on the television.

Her eyes sparkled watching them run, pass, and shoot.

"REMARKABLE," she whispered.

Rose made her own ball out of paper and string and kicked it around the neighborhood alone.

Her father shook his finger at her, scolding, "Girls don't play soccer, Rose. Go do your chores."

Her teachers agreed. "Stop dreaming, Rose. Focus on your books."

Each night, Rose sat on her bed,
reshaping her soccer ball.

When she played soccer, she felt strong.
The game was in her bones.

Rose fell asleep, clutching her ball,
dreaming of kicking the winning goal
in a big soccer match.

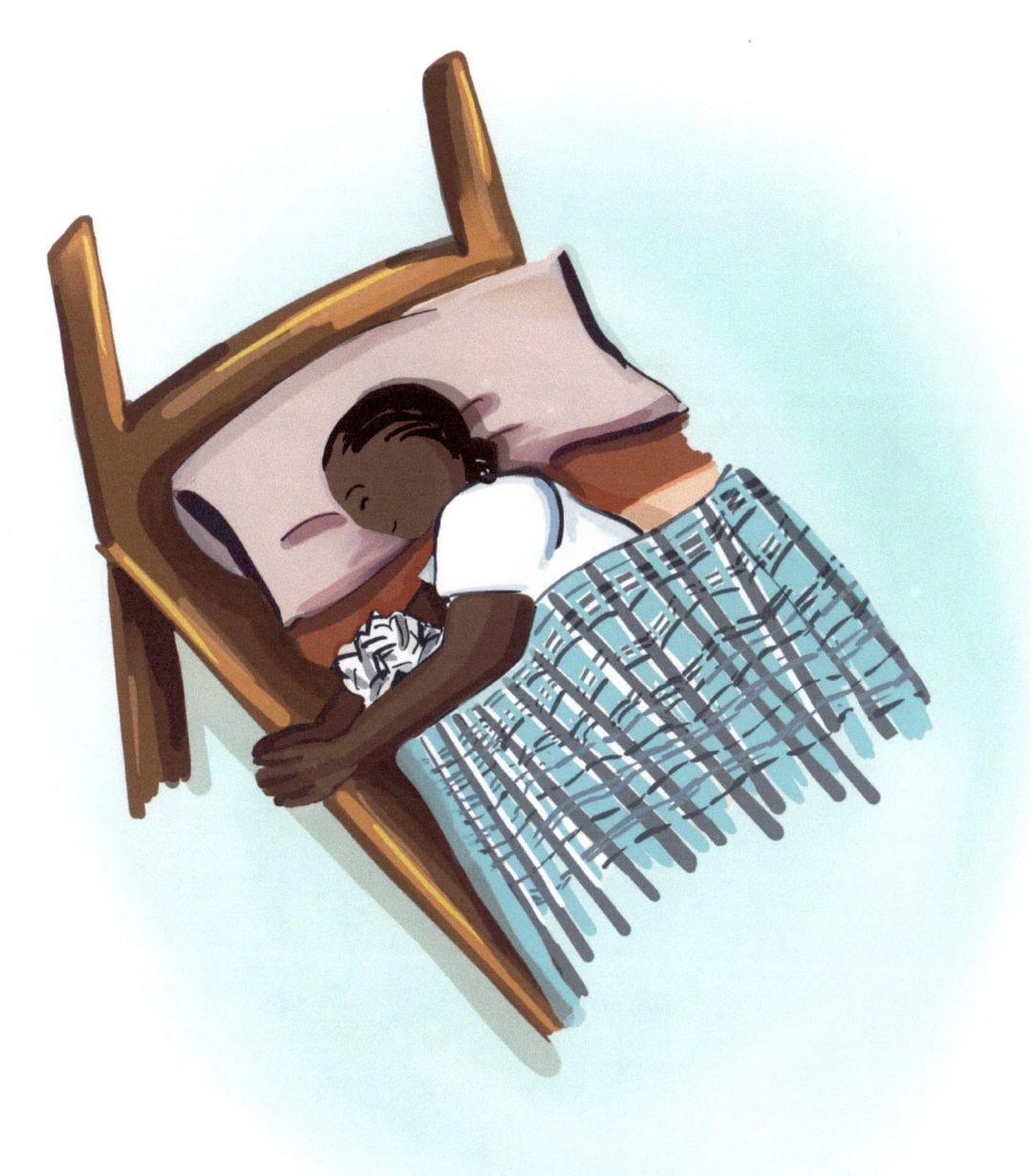

A man named Abdul loved soccer, too.

His grandmother raised him to believe that girls can do anything boys can do.

He saw girls running around Kibera by themselves kicking balls of paper and string. Their eyes sparkled while they played.

When he saw the boys keeping the girls off the soccer pitch, he got an idea.

One day, Rose ran past Abdul, kicking her ball.

"REMARKABLE," he thought and approached her, smiling.

"I'm starting a girls' soccer team here in Kibera. Do you want to play?"

Her heart leapt, but she hesitated. Rose recognized him from the neighborhood, and she longed to play with other girls, but she remembered how the boys made her feel. She thought about what her parents and teachers said.

"Maybe." She looked down at her fidgeting feet. "I mean, I think so."

Abdul saw the excitement in her body and the doubt behind her eyes. "Come to the field tomorrow and see for yourself. It's going to be great."

Turning toward home,
Rose dropped the ball at her feet and started dribbling it slowly.

Then **FASTER** and **FASTER**.

By the time she reached home, she was gleaming with sweat.

Feeling brave and proud she whispered, "I **LOVE** this game."

"Rose, where have you been?
Come help with dinner!" her mom called.

While preparing vegetables for the stew, Rose's hands shook, her breath quickened, her foot tapped impatiently. She didn't want to upset her parents. But she thought, "How can I stay home when I was made to play soccer?"

That night, Rose

TOSSED

The next morning, Rose thought about the women from across the world playing soccer on TV. She stared at the ball resting between her feet until she couldn't sit still any longer.

She took a deep breath and stood up. She walked to the pitch with her paper ball under her arm and butterflies in her stomach.

When Rose turned the corner, she could barely believe the scene in front of her.

The pitch was full of **REMARKABLE** girls just like her running, kicking, and playing. Their eyes sparkled. Abdul spotted her and waved her over.

Rose ran to join the girls, a smile as wide as the sun spreading across her face.

Author's Note

Rose Achieng grew up in Kibera, in the heart of Nairobi, Kenya. She first played for Girls Soccer in Kibera with Abdul Kassim in 2002. There were no girls' teams to play against in Kibera, so they took on the boys. At first, they lost badly. 5-0. 4-0.

Then, one day, they beat the boys. Their confidence grew immediately, and they entered into bigger Nairobi tournaments. They didn't have fancy jerseys, nice fields, or big buses like some of their opponents. Yet undaunted, with the help of Rose's biting penalty kicks, the Kibera girls started winning those games, too.

Rose used her soccer skills to change people's minds about what girls could do. That gave her and her teammates the audacity to dream bigger. They wanted to go to school. Few families in Kibera could afford high school tuition, and if they could only send one child, families often chose to send a boy.

In 2006, Abdul opened Kibera Girls Soccer Academy (KGSA) for his soccer players. What started out as an informal school for the team quickly became a two-story building with 130 students. They offered opportunities in other sports as well as after school clubs for the girls who didn't play soccer, but the soccer program continued to be a huge contributor to KGSA's success. Rose was part of KGSA's inaugural class.

Rose worked hard in school and continued to thrive in soccer. In 2011, Abdul invited both Zainab Khamis ("Commando") and Rose to try out for the Kenyan Homeless World Cup Team. It was the first time Kenya sent a women's team. After a rigorous tryout, both girls were selected for the team. They flew to Paris, France to compete. "They have two legs. We have two legs," Rose reminded her nervous teammates. "Let's go play." And they did. They beat France, the Netherlands, the United States, and Brazil. The girls from Kenya impressed everyone. In the championship game against Mexico, it was tied 3-3. Rose scored the fourth and deciding goal. The Kenyan women won the 2011 Homeless World Cup.

KGSA continues to thrive offering free high school education, nutrition, health care, extracurricular activities and leadership initiatives to 130+ girls every year. The school supports graduates with college scholarships and recently opened a dormitory with a turf soccer pitch on the roof. KGSA is working to break the cycle of poverty for the girls and their families, empowering them to become stronger, more independent and resilient women.

In 2019, KGSA's senior soccer team made it to the Kenyan Women's Premier League. Rose was the captain of the team.

Rose continues to be instrumental in creating a stronger, more resilient Kibera. She works hard so that her two daughters have a stable childhood and know that they, too, are remarkable.

For more information about Rose and KGSA, read *Play Like a Girl* and visit www.kgsafoundation.org.

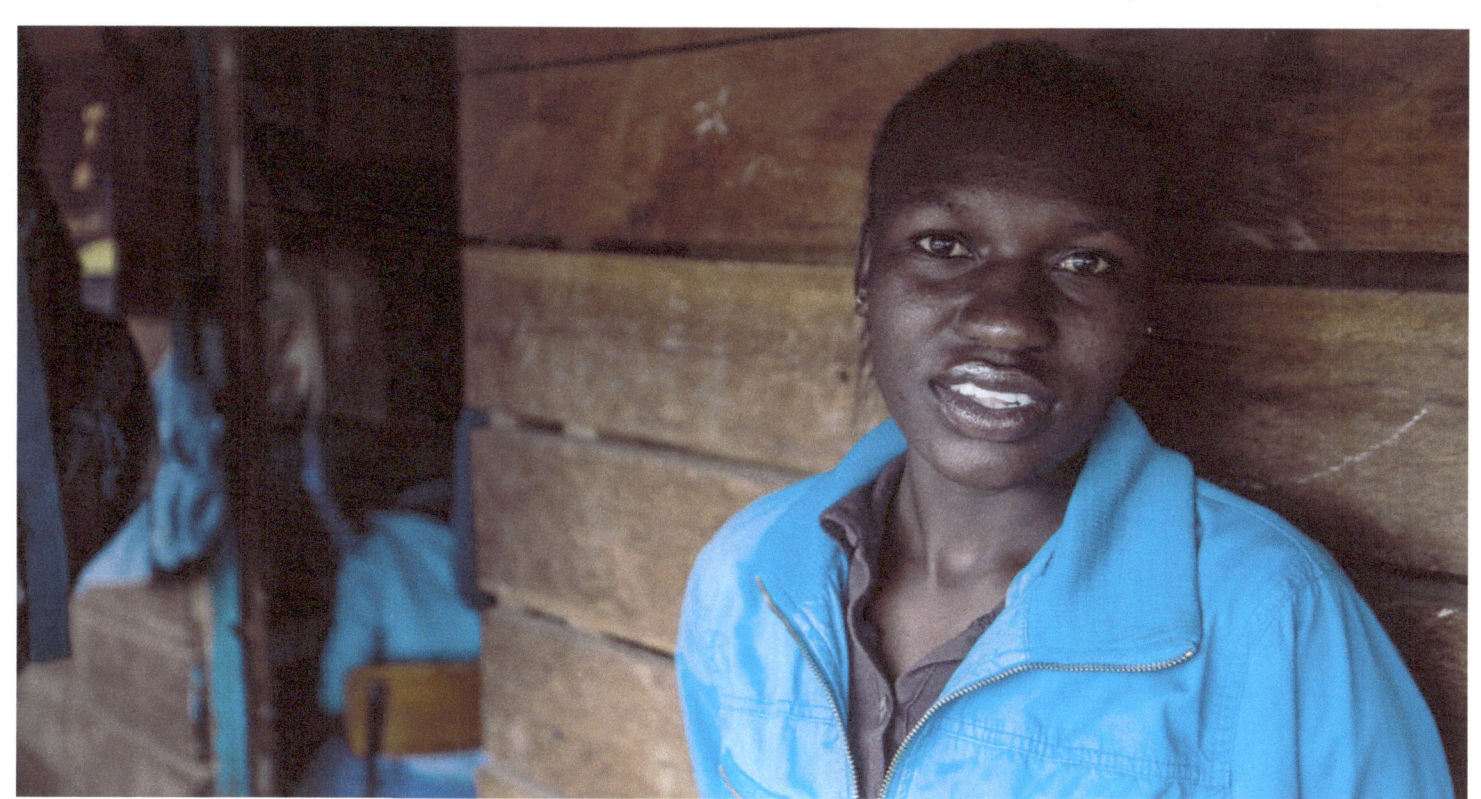

Photo by Jake Naughton

Remarkable Rose Achieng

ISBN: 979-8-218-12985-9
Text Copyright © 2023 Ellie Roscher | Illustrations Copyright © 2023 Lily Banning

All Rights Reserved. No portion of this book may be reproduced, stored in a retrieval system, or transmitted in any form or by any means, mechanical, electronic, photocopying, recording, or otherwise, without written permission from the author.

Dedicated to Rose, her teammates, and the girls of Kibera Girls Soccer Academy who are transforming Kibera through play.

Ellie Roscher was taken by Rose's story right away when she heard it while teaching a gender equity unit to high schoolers in 2010. She traveled to Kenya in 2012 and 2013 to interview Rose and the other students at KGSA, which became the book *Play Like a Girl*. Ellie is also the author of *The Embodied Path*, *12 Tiny Things*, and *How Coffee Saved My Life*. She holds an MFA in writing from Sarah Lawrence College and an MA in theology from Luther Seminary. She teaches writing, yoga, and embodiment in Minneapolis and online. Find out more at ellieroscher.com and @ellieroscher.

Lily Banning is a visual artist whose varied portfolio includes oil paintings, illustrations, public murals and textiles. She is an alumna of Washington DC's 202Creates residency program and was a featured panelist at the Emerging Arts Leaders Symposium in 2017. Her work has been exhibited at the Hill Center Gallery, Watergate Gallery and Torpedo Factory in the Washington, D.C. area and Universita' Ca' Foscari in Venice, Italy. Lily lives in Portland, Oregon with her husband and pup. Follow along @art.lilyb and www.lilybanning.art.

Printed in the USA
CPSIA information can be obtained
at www.ICGtesting.com
LVHW072328250823
756276LV00002B/43